DINOSAURS!

PARASAUROLOPHUS
AND OTHER DUCK-BILLED AND
BEAKED HERBIVORES

by
David West

Gareth Stevens
Publishing

Please visit our Web site, www.garethstevens.com.
For a free color catalog of all our high-quality books,
call toll free 1-800-542-2595 or fax 1-877-542-2596.

Library of Congress Cataloging-in-Publication Data

West, David, 1956-
Parasaurolophus and other duck-billed and beaked herbivores / by David West.
p. cm. — (Dinosaurs!)
Includes index.
ISBN 978-1-4339-4228-0 (pbk.)
ISBN 978-1-4339-4229-7 (6 pack)
ISBN 978-1-4339-4227-3 (lib. bdg.)
1. Herbivores, Fossil—Juvenile literature. 2. Parasaurolophus—Juvenile literature. I. Title.
QE862.O65W445 2011
567.9—dc22
2010011540

First Edition

Published in 2011 by
Gareth Stevens Publishing
111 East 14th Street, Suite 349
New York, NY 10003

Copyright © 2011 David West Books

Designed by David West Books
Editor: Ronne Randall

Printed in China

CPSIA compliance information: Batch #DS10GS: For further information contact Gareth Stevens, New York, New York at 1-800-542-2595.

Contents

The dinosaurs here are of three different types. Parasaurolophus *is a* **hadrosaurid**, *Iguanodon is an* **iguanodont**, *and Lesothosaurus is an* **ornithopod**.

SELF DEFENSE
With the exception of the iguanodonts' thumb spikes (see pp. 12–13), these dinosaurs had no defense against **predators**, relying on herding to provide safety in numbers. The smaller ornithopods used speed to escape their attackers.

What Are Duck-Billed and Beaked **Herbivores**?

Duck-billed dinosaurs belonged to the family hadrosauridae, whose members were plant eaters with duck-shaped beaks. They were related to iguanodontian dinosaurs and had similar body layouts. Along with iguanodonts and hadrosaurids, smaller beaked dinosaurs are included to make up the group known as ornithopods.

Dinosaurs lived throughout the Mesozoic Era, which is divided into three periods, shown here. It is sometimes called the Age of the Reptiles. Dinosaurs first appeared in the Upper Triassic period and died out during a **mass extinction event** *65 million years ago.*

CRESTS

Hadrosaurids are divided into two subfamilies. The lambeosaurines had hollow head crests and were generally less bulky. The hadrosaurines, like *Maiasaura* (see pp. 18–19), had no crests and were usually larger.

Parasaurolophus

BILLS AND BEAKS

Hadrosaurids had beaks that looked like a duck's bill, which is why they are called duck-billed dinosaurs. Iguanodonts and the smaller ornithopods had narrow skulls with a toothless beak that was covered in a hornlike material called keratin. At the back of the jaws were **batteries** of teeth for mashing up the tough plants they fed on.

Iguanodon

Lesothosaurus

FOUR- OR TWO-LEGGED

The bulky hadrosaurids and iguanodonts could walk on two or four legs. The smaller ornithopods were two-legged and very quick in order to escape predators.

SIZE

Both duckbills and iguanodonts grew to enormous sizes. *Iguanodon* would have reached 29 feet (8.8 m), and *Parasaurolophus* could grow to 31 feet (9.4 m). *Lesothosaurus* was only 3.3 feet (1 m).

	227	205	180	159	144		98		65 Millions of years ago (mya)
	Upper	Lower	Middle	Upper		Lower		Upper	
	TRIASSIC		JURASSIC			CRETACEOUS			

Altirhinus

Altirhinus means "high nose." It was closely related to *Iguanodon* (see pp. 12–13). *Altirhinus* differed from *Iguanodon* only in that it had more teeth, a flatter, wider bill, and a very curved nose.

The arched nose of *Altirhinus* may have been able to expand for **courtship** display, as in modern-day **elephant seals**. *Altirhinus* was two-legged when walking or running, but probably became four-legged when feeding from the ground. The three middle fingers of its hand

A group of Altirhinuses feed on the few plants at the edge of a desert in this scene from *Lower Cretaceous Asia. A herd of Altirhinus* can be seen in the background, **migrating** *to greener feeding grounds.*

were wide and ended in hooflike bones, suggesting that they were used for walking. The outside fingers were different. The first finger was a sharp spike, as on *Iguanodon*. Besides defense, the thumb spike might also have been used for breaking the shells of seeds or fruit. The fifth finger may have been useful for grasping food. *Altirhinus* could crop with its beak while chewing with its teeth.

Altirhinus was about 28 feet (8.5 m) long and weighed around 4 tons (3.6 metric tons).

Corythosaurus

Corythosaurus was a type of duck-billed or hadrosaurid dinosaur called a lambeosaurine. Its name means "helmet lizard," referring to the large semicircular crest growing up from its head. It was closely related to *Lambeosaurus* and *Olorotitan* (see pp. 20–21), although their crests were very different.

Like other duck-billed dinosaurs, it had a toothless beak, which it used to pluck plant leaves and stems. The back of the jaws contained

8

A group of Corythosauruses *make their way to a water hole in this scene from Upper Cretaceous North America. A male calls out a signal using his crest to* **amplify** *the sound. Males might have had colored crests for courtship display.*

hundreds of small teeth. These were used to crush and grind plants. When a tooth wore down, it was replaced by a newly grown tooth. As with other lambeosaurines, *Corythosaurus*'s crest contained air passages that were connected to its nose and lungs. They made sounds like a loud wind instrument that might have been used at times of danger.

Corythosaurus grew up to 35 feet (10.7 m) long and weighed around 4 tons (3.6 metric tons).

9

Gryposaurus

Gryposaurus, meaning "hooked-nose lizard" because of
the shape of its nose, was one of the most widely
spread and longest-lived hadrosaurids. These dinosaurs
lived across the entire North American continent for
five million years.

This dinosaur gets its name from the distinctive bony bump on its
nose. The roughened texture of the bump suggests that it may have
been used to butt other males during mating competitions.

10

A herd of Gryposauruses *crosses a narrow river to better feeding grounds, while a pair of* Chirostenotes *look on in this scene from Upper Cretaceous North America. A male* Gryposaurus *in the foreground shows off his colored nose in a courtship **ritual**.*

A cast taken from fossilized remains shows that the skin on its neck, sides, and belly was covered with smooth scales less than a quarter of an inch (0.6 cm) in size. *Gryposaurus* had a huge array of 300 teeth, which were replaced when they wore out. Scientists think it was able to eat any type of plants, using its beak to rip away tough stems while its teeth mashed food into a pulp.

Gryposaurus was about 33 feet (10 m) long and weighed up to 3 tons (2.7 metric tons).

Lower Cretaceous,140–110 mya
Belgium, France, Germany, Spain,
United Kingdom, United States

Iguanodon

Iguanodon means "iguana tooth," because its teeth looked like those of an iguana. It was one of the earliest dinosaur **fossils** to be discovered, even before the name "dinosaur" was used. An early mistake in reconstruction placed its thumb spike on its nose!

Iguanodon's body structure was quite similar to that of its later relatives, the hadrosaurids. It could shift from walking on two legs to walking on four. Its arms were long and strong, with hands that had three central

Its thumb spikes useless against the fast-moving predators, a sickly Iguanodon *struggles to stay on its feet as a pack of* Deinonychuses *snap and slash at it in this scene from Lower Cretaceous North America.*

fingers ending in hooves that could bear weight. The thumbs were conical spikes that stuck out and were possibly used as defensive weapons. The little finger was long and could have been used to hold plants while feeding. The front end of the snout was like a beak that was used to crop plants. The many broad teeth in the back of the jaw mashed up the plants.

Iguanodon grew up to 29 feet (8.8 m) long and weighed around 3.5 tons (3.2 metric tons).

Leaellynasaura

Leaellynasaura was named after the daughter of the **paleontologist** who discovered it. Its fossils were found in southeastern Australia, but when *Leaellynasaura* was alive, the continent was much farther south, inside the Antarctic Circle.

Leaellynasaura was a small ornithopod dinosaur that weighed slightly more than a child. It lived in Antarctica, where, for part of the year, there was no sunlight. The climate was warmer 110 million years ago,

14

A pair of Leaellynasauras run back to their burrows across sandy dunes near the coast of a Lower Cretaceous South Polar continent. The sun barely rises above the horizon as the long dark days of winter approach.

but was still relatively cold, especially during the dark days of winter. The eyes of *Leaellynasaura* were huge, and the part of the brain controlling sight was large. This suggests it was well **adapted** to living in a dark environment. Scientists think it may have been warm-blooded, since there are no modern, cold-blooded reptiles living in arctic environments.

Leaellynasaura grew to about 7 feet (2.1 m) long and weighed up to 36 pounds (16.3 kg).

Lesothosaurus

Lesothosaurus, meaning "Lesotho lizard," was named after the country its fossils were found in. It had short arms, a long tail, and long legs that made it a fast runner. Like other ornithopods, it needed to be speedy to escape predators such as *Syntarsus*.

Lesothosaurus had a small beak with which to crop tough plants. Behind the beak, it had flat, triangular-shaped teeth that interlocked. These were good for chewing up the plants it fed on.

A group of Lesothosauruses *scatter across a sandy beach to escape a speedy* **carnivorous** Syntarsus *in this coastal scene from Upper Triassic Africa. Parts of* Lesothosaurus's *skeleton were hollow, indicating that it was a light and fast dinosaur.*

The skeleton of *Lesothosaurus* was light. Its leg and arm bones were hollow, and there were hollow spaces in the skull. The front limbs were small, and the hands each had four big fingers and a smaller fifth finger, which were probably used for grasping plants while it ate. While browsing on plants, *Lesothosaurus* might occasionally stand upright and scan the landscape for prowling predators.

Lesothosaurus grew up to 3.3 feet (1 m) long and weighed little more than 13 pounds (6 kg).

17

Maiasaura

Maiasaura, meaning "caring mother lizard," was a large hadrosaurine with a flat, wide beak. It was named after nests were discovered with remains of eggshells and babies too large to be **hatchlings**. This suggested that these giant dinosaurs raised their young.

Herds of *Maiasauras* built nesting **colonies** that were packed closely together, like those of seabirds today. The nests were made of soil, with a gap between them of around 23 feet (7 m), less than the length

In this scene from Upper Cretaceous North America, a nesting colony of Maiasauras includes hatchlings scampering about while others are being fed in their nest by their parents. An approaching sandstorm threatens to bury the colony.

of the adult dinosaur. The eggs were laid in a circular pattern, up to 30 or 40 at a time. Fossils of baby *Maiasauras* show that they were unable to walk when they first hatched. Fossils also show that their teeth were partly worn, which means that the adults fed them in the nest. They had large eyes and a short snout, giving them a cute appearance—a common feature among animals that rely on their parents.

Maiasaura grew up to 30 feet (9.1 m) long and weighed up to 4 tons (3.6 metric tons).

19

Upper Cretaceous
70–65 mya
Russia

Olorotitan

Olorotitan, meaning "gigantic swan," was named for its long, swanlike neck. It is the most complete hadrosaur fossil ever to be found outside North America. It had an unusual crest in the shape of a fan growing out of the back of its head.

Like *Corythosaurus* (see pp. 8–9), *Olorotitan* used its crest both as a sound instrument and as a device to attract females during courtship. Like other lambeosaurines, it had a beak to pluck plants and a battery

A group of Olorotitans have moved down to a pool fed by a waterfall in this scene from Upper Cretaceous Asia. Places such as these, with the **potential** for sudden flooding, were ideal for the fossilization of dead animals as they quickly became buried in silt.

of teeth at the back of its jaw to crush the food before swallowing. *Olorotitan* was closely related to the North American lambeosaurines *Corythosaurus* and *Hypacrosaurus*. Scientists think that these lambeosaurines originally came from the area we know as Asia and migrated to North America before the large landmass split into several continents.

Olorotitan grew to 39 feet (11.9 m) and weighed about 2.2 tons (2 metric tons).

21

Ouranosaurus

Ouranosaurus means "brave lizard." It was very strange looking, with tall spines growing from its back. Scientists think these may have supported a hump like a camel's or a sail-like structure. The sail would have helped regulate its body temperature in a warm climate.

Paleontologists think that *Ouranosaurus* lived in a harsh, almost desertlike environment and was closely related to *Iguanodon* (see pp. 12–13). They had many similar features, such as a thumb spike, which

22

Three Ouranosauruses, *who have become separated from their herd, make their way across a rocky desert in search of green feeding grounds in this scene from Lower Cretaceous Africa. One* Ouranosaurus *stops to call out to its lost herd.*

was smaller on *Ouranosaurus*. Its wrist was large, and the bones were fused together, which made it stronger when walking. The second and third fingers were broad and hooflike, and the last outside finger was long and probably used for holding leaves and twigs. It had an unusual head, and its snout, which was much longer than *Iguanodon*'s, ended in a beak.

Ouranosaurus was about 23 feet (7 m) long and weighed around 2.7 tons (2.4 metric tons).

Parasaurolophus

Parasaurolophus means "like *Saurolophus*" (see pp. 26–27). It was a lambeosaurine, and its most noticeable feature was its long head crest. There are three species, all with different-sized crests. *Parasaurolophus walkeri*, shown here, had the longest crest.

There were many theories about the crest's function. One was that it was used as a snorkel to help with underwater breathing. This has now been rejected, since there is no hole at the end of the crest. It is

24

In a scene from Upper Cretaceous North America, a herd of Parasaurolophuses *moves on from a water hole. The male* Parasaurolophuses *are reddening and using their head crests to sing in a courtship contest.*

believed that the head crest may have had several uses. It was used as a visual display for identifying species and sex. Hollow tubes inside suggest that it was also used to amplify sound. These duckbills also had good hearing, and experiments have shown that adults were sensitive to the high frequencies a **juvenile** might produce. It has also been suggested that the crest may have been used to keep the brain cool.

Parasaurolophus was about 31 feet (9.4 m) long and weighed up to 6 tons (5.4 metric tons).

Upper Cretaceous
74–70 mya
Canada, Mongolia

Saurolophus

Saurolophus, or "crested lizard," was a large hadrosaurine dinosaur. It is one of the few dinosaurs found on more than one continent. It is recognized by a spikelike crest that sticks up and back from its head. Like all hadrosaurs, it could walk on four or two legs.

As with *Parasaurolophus* (see pp. 24–25), the head crest might have had several functions. Fossils were found in the Horseshoe Canyon Formation, close to the **encroaching** Western Interior Seaway, the

As rolling waves crash against a headland, a group of Saurolophuses make their way along the rocky shore of the Western Interior Seaway of Upper Cretaceous North America. In the background, Pteranodons glide above the waves in search of fish.

shallow sea that covered the midsection of North America through much of the Cretaceous period. *Saurolophus* lived with hadrosaurids *Edmontosaurus* and hollow-crested *Hypacrosaurus*, **hypsilophodont** *Parksosaurus*, **ankylosaurid** *Euoplocephalus*, **nodosaurid** *Edmontonia*, horned dinosaur *Pachyrhinosaurus*, **pachycephalosaurid** *Stegoceras*, and the ostrich-mimic *Ornithomimus*.

Saurolophus grew up to 39 feet (11.9 m) long and weighed around 2.1 tons (1.9 metric tons).

27

Velafrons

Velafrons, meaning "sailed forehead," is a newly named dinosaur whose fossil remains were recently discovered in Mexico. It was a large plant eater belonging to the lambeosaurine family of duckbills.

Velafrons lived in a humid estuary near the southernmost tip of Laramidia, a part of western America at the edge of the Western Interior Seaway. It was an area where salt water from the ocean mixed with freshwater from rivers. Many of the fossilized dinosaur bones

28

In this scene from Upper Cretaceous western America, a pair of Velafronses are caught by a large wave as a giant storm brews up out to sea. Whole herds of dinosaurs could be wiped out by these **catastrophic** storms.

discovered with *Velafrons* are covered with fossilized snails and marine clams, suggesting that *Velafrons* lived near the shore. The region was sometimes hit by huge, violent storms that affected miles of coastline and killed off entire herds of dinosaurs. Scientists think that *Velafrons*'s crest would have been used as a musical instrument for attracting females.

Velafrons grew up to 35.7 feet (10.9 m) long and weighed up to 1.8 tons (1.6 metric tons).

Animal Gallery

Other dinosaurs and animals that appear in the scenes.

Pteranodon (pp. 26–27)
"toothless flyer"
pterosaur (flying reptile)
Upper Cretaceous
United States

Deinonychus (p. 13)
"terrible claw"
carnivorous
dromaeosaurid
(vicious **raptor**)
Lower Cretaceous
United States

Chirostenotes
(pp. 10–11)
"narrow-handed"
oviraptorosaur
(beaked, feathered raptor)
Upper Cretaceous
Canada

Syntarsus (pp. 16–17)
"fused ankle"
theropod (two-legged
carnivorous dinosaur)
Upper Triassic
South Africa, United States,
Zimbabwe

Glossary

adapted Changed to cope with a different condition or situation.

amplify To make a sound louder.

ankylosaurid A member of the ankylosauridae family of armored dinosaurs that includes *Ankylosaurus*.

batteries Rows or a grouping in lines.

carnivorous Meat eating.

catastrophic Violent and destructive.

colonies Groups of animals of the same species that live closely with each other.

courtship Mate-selection rituals.

dromaeosaurid A member of a group of carnivorous dinosaurs known as raptors, with slashing claws on their feet.

elephant seals Elephant seals take their name from the large inflating nose of the adult males, which looks like a short elephant's trunk.

encroaching Moving over boundaries, as when deserts encroach on grassland.

fossils The remains of living things that have turned to rock.

hadrosaurid A member of the family of duck-billed dinosaurs called *hadrosauridae*.

hatchling The newborn animal that emerges from a hard-shelled egg.

herbivore A plant eater.

hypsilophodont A member of a family of fast, herbivorous, small, two-legged ornithopod dinosaurs.

iguanodont A member of the plant-eating dinosaurs that include *Iguanodon*.

juvenile A young dinosaur.

mass extinction event A large-scale disappearance of animal and plant species over a relatively short period of time.

migrating Moving from one place to another, either for a short seasonal period, or forever.

nodosaurid A member of a family of ankylosaurian dinosaurs.

ornithopod A member of the ornithopoda family of bird-hipped dinosaurs that became one of the most successful groups of plant-eating dinosaurs in the Cretaceous world.

pachycephalosaurid A member of a family of bone-headed dinosaurs that includes *Pachycephalosaurus*.

paleontologist A scientist who studies the forms of life that existed in earlier geological periods by looking at fossils.

potential To have the possibility.

predators Animals that hunt and kill other animals for food.

pterosaur A member of the flying reptiles that lived during the age of the dinosaurs.

raptors Members of the family dromaeosauridae, such as *Deinonychus*.

rituals A series of special acts or ways of doing something.

theropod A member of a two-legged dinosaur family that includes most of the giant carnivorous dinosaurs.

Index